PRIOR KNOWLEDGE:

THE STORY OF AFRICA

SERIES

Younger's
Revised Edition

I0528742

Get Your FREE Len Eddy's World Adventures Activity Book!

Join our reader family and receive a fun-filled activity book inspired by Len Eddy's World Adventures—completely free!

Packed with coloring pages, puzzles, and learning games, it's the perfect companion to the series.

Scan the QR code below to sign up and claim your activity book!

Let the adventure continue beyond the pages!

Copyright © 2025 by Len Eddy's Press, LLC. All rights reserved.
No part of this book may be reproduced, distributed, or transmitted in any form or by any means, including photocopying, recording, or other electronic or mechanical methods, without the prior written permission of the publisher, except in the case of brief quotations embodied in critical reviews and certain other noncommercial uses permitted by copyright law. For permission requests, please write to the publisher at the address below:

Len Eddy's Press, LLC
www.leneddyspressllc.com
info@leneddyspressllc.com
Attention: Permissions Desk
9490 FM 1960 Bypass Road West, Suite 200-175
Humble, TX
77338
USA

Written by Rhonda Bady-Hill
Edited by Sharon Kleinman
Illustrated by Samantha (Sami) Collins
Cover Design by Samantha (Sami) Collins

ISBN Print: 978-1-967907-10-6

Revised Edition published in the United States of America in 2025 by
Len Eddy's Press, LLC.

Hi! I'm Len Eddy.

I'm a young lion cub from Africa. I love to explore new places and learn about the world.

Let me tell you a story about my home,

AFRICA.

HOW IT ALL BEGAN

A long time ago, about 200 million years ago, the Earth was one big piece of land called **PANGAEA** [PAN-JEE-UH].

Then, one day, there was a loud **CRACK!** The big land began to split and break apart. The pieces moved away slowly. One of those pieces became **AFRICA.**

PANGAEA

CONTINENTAL DRIFT

BEFORE

The **EARTH** shook, and the oceans splashed as the land moved apart. Mountains and rivers started to form.

AFTER

Slowly, everything started to change, and **AFRICA** began to look like it does today.

NATURE

AFRICA is huge! It is about four times the size of the United States. It is full of wonders.

In the beginning, **AFRICA** was flat and empty. No trees, rivers, or animals. But slowly, nature changed it. Mountains rose up, rivers flowed, and jungles grew.

DESERTS also formed, like the Sahara [Suh-har-uh], the biggest hot desert on Earth. It is so big that it covers an area the size of the United States!

Africa also has **RAINFORESTS.** They are green, wet, and full of life. Tall trees make a roof called the canopy, and under this roof, it is dark and quiet. Many animals live there, like chimpanzees, gorillas, and colorful birds.

The trees grow so close together that the sunlight barely reaches the ground. The animals love it here because it is cool and safe.

Between the deserts and rainforests are the **SAVANNAS.**

Savannas are wide grasslands. This is where elephants, giraffes, zebras, and lions like me live.

The **SUNSETS** on the savanna are bright red, yellow, pink, and orange. It looks like a painting. Tall yellow grasses sway in the wind, and acacia trees spread their branches like umbrellas.

There are also tall mountains, like Mount Kilimanjaro [KIL-LUH-MUHN-JAA-ROW]. It is the highest mountain in **AFRICA.** It is very hard to climb! It has snow at the top, even though it is close to the equator, where it is usually hot. Many people try to climb it, but it takes a lot of strength and courage.

ANIMALS

AFRICA is home to many animals. There are over 2,600 kinds of birds and 1,100 kinds of mammals!

The cheetah is one of the fastest animals on Earth. It can run as fast as a car! And the peregrine [PER-I-GRIN] falcon is even faster when it dives. It is like a roller coaster!

In the **RAINFORESTS,** monkeys swing from tree to tree, and in the rivers, you can find hippos and crocodiles. Africa is truly full of amazing creatures, big and small.

AFRICAN ELEPHANT is the largest land animal in the world. It can weigh as much as a school bus! Elephants are very smart and live in family groups. They use their trunks to grab food, drink water, and even hug each other.

GIRAFFES, with their long necks, eat leaves from the tops of trees that other animals can't reach. Every animal has its own special way to survive.

THE CRADLE OF HUMANITY

AFRICA is not just about nature. It is also the first home of humans.

Long ago, the first humans lived here. One of them was named **"LUCY"** by scientists. Lucy used her strong arms to climb trees to stay safe and find food.

Early humans lived in small groups. They worked together to hunt, gather food, and survive.

They were called **HUNTER-GATHERERS.** They used sharp stones as tools and learned to make fire to stay warm. Later, they started farming and building villages.

These villages grew bigger, and people did different jobs like farming, building, and trading. They shared everything they had and helped each other survive. It was the beginning of human life as we know it.

KINGDOMS AND EMPIRE

Over time, big **KINGDOMS** grew in Africa. There was Egypt, with its pyramids and pharaohs. The pyramids were giant stone tombs built for their kings. The Egyptians [IH-JIP-SHUHNS] also built temples and wrote using picture symbols called

HIEROGLYPHS. There was the Kingdom of Kush, with its gold and bustling cities. People in Kush [KOOSH] were known for their beautiful jewelry and their strong warriors.

There was also the Kingdom of Aksum [AHK-SOOM], famous for trade and tall stone towers called obelisks. Traders from all over came to Aksum to buy gold, ivory, and spices. And there was the Mali Kingdom, led by a kind ruler named Mansa Musa who shared his gold with many people. He was known as the richest man in history! He helped build schools and made sure that his people learned and grew.

In these **KINGDOMS,** people lived in busy cities with markets full of traders. There were farmers, builders, artists, and teachers. Everyone worked together to make their kingdoms strong and beautiful.

GEOGRAPHY

AFRICA is like a giant island with **OCEANS** on almost every side. There are four big waters: the Atlantic Ocean, the Mediterranean [MED-I-TUH-REY-NEE-UHN] Sea, the Red Sea, and the Indian Ocean. If you traveled all around Africa, you would see oceans and seas almost everywhere!

There are also big **RIVERS.** The Nile is the longest river in the world. It flows through many countries and brings water to dry lands. People have lived along the Nile for thousands of years. They grow crops like wheat and vegetables along its banks. The Niger River is also important, helping kingdoms grow rich from trade. Rivers in Africa are like highways, helping people move from place to place.

AFRICA has many natural treasures, like gold and salt. Salt was very valuable long ago, even more than gold! People used salt to keep their food fresh. Ivory, made from elephant tusks, was also valuable, but many elephants were hunted because of this, which was very sad.

SAD TIMES

AFRICA has a sad part of its history too. Long ago, explorers from Europe came to Africa looking for riches. They started taking people from Africa to work as **SLAVES** in faraway lands. This was called the Transatlantic Slave Trade. It was a terrible time. Many families were torn apart. People were taken from their homes and forced to work without pay. They were treated very badly, but the spirit of Africa stayed strong.

Some of the people who were taken showed great **COURAGE.** They sang songs to stay strong, told stories about their homeland, and kept their culture alive, even in the hardest times. Their bravery and strength helped them survive, and their stories are still told today.

CONCLUSION

AFRICA is a land of beauty, strength, and courage. Today, Africa has 54 countries, each with its own culture and history. Over 1 billion people live here. They speak many different languages, celebrate colorful festivals, and have wonderful traditions. Africa is full of music, dance, and stories that bring people together.

Maybe one day, you will visit **AFRICA** and see all its wonders! You could see the tall mountains, wide savannas, deep rainforests, and the amazing animals that live here.

THE END

Now, are you ready for an adventure? In the next story, we will learn more about the time of slavery and the strength of the people during that dark time.

Come join me!

QUESTIONS FOR YOUNGER'S

1. What was the earth called 200 million years ago?

_____

2. How much bigger is Africa than the United States?

_____

3. What river is the longest river in the world?

_____

4. Name some of the animals that live on the Savanna.

_____

5. Name some of the animals that live in the rainforest.

_____

6. How many animals call Africa home?

_____

7. Which animal is the fastest on Earth?

_____

8. How did early humans survive?

_____

9. Who is believed to be the richest man in history?

_____

10. Name 2 of Africa's natural treasures.

_____

11. What was a sad part of Africa's history?

_____

12. How many countries does Africa have?

_____

ANSWERS FOR YOUNGER'S

1. A Pangaea. The Pangaea cracked and split up!

2. Africa is 4 times the size of the United States.

3. The Nile River

4. Elephants, Giraffes, Zebras, and Lions

5. Chimpanzees, Gorillas, and Birds

6. Over 2,600 Birds and 1,100 Mammals

7. Cheetah

8. Early humans worked together to survive.

9. Mansa Musa, the Ruler of Mali

10. Gold and Salt

11. The Transatlantic Slave Trade

12. Africa has 54 countries.

REFERENCES:

www.kids.mongabay.com

www.psychologytoday.com

www.livescience.com

www.ducksters.com

www.history.com

www.lonelyplanet.com,

www.differencebetween.net

www.quora.com

www.roomforafrica.com

www.worldatlas.com

www.cotf.edu

www.blueplanetbiomes.org

www.blackhistorystudies.com

www.reference.com

www.britanica.com

www.istrockphoto.com

www.canva.com

ABOUT THE AUTHOR

My name is Rhonda Bady-Hill. I'm a storyteller, public speaker, voice-over artist, singer, actress, writer, world traveler, and mother of three amazing children. My kids had the privilege of attending a K-8 school with an exceptional history program that was sometimes interactive and engaging and went far beyond the basics.

As I traveled to schools across the U.S. leading storytelling workshops, I noticed that many students didn't seem deeply connected to history, especially when creating their own stories. That observation stayed with me. I wondered if children were exposed to the rich histories of indigenous peoples and ancient civilizations at a younger age and more regularly, how much more empathy, imagination, and curiosity they could carry into the world?

I've known for many years that I would write children's books one day, and that a lion or lion cub would be the heart of the adventure. Eventually, I discovered who that lion was: a wide-eyed, wonder-filled cub named Len Eddy.

Get Your FREE Len Eddy's World Adventures Activity Book!

Join our reader family and receive a fun-filled activity book inspired by Len Eddy's World Adventures—completely free!

Packed with coloring pages, puzzles, and learning games, it's the perfect companion to the series.

Scan the QR code below to sign up and claim your activity book!

Let the adventure continue beyond the pages!

"COME EXPERIENCE THE MAGIC OF SEEING THRU WORDS"

Len Eddy's World Adventures
Len Eddy's Press, LLC
9490 FM 1960 Bypass Rd West
Suite 200-175
Humble, TX 77338
info@leneddyspressllc.com
571-899-2590
www.leneddyspressllc.com

www.ingramcontent.com/pod-product-compliance
Lightning Source LLC
Chambersburg PA
CBHW041459120626
46547CB00003B/480